ISBN: 978-1-7355864-9-6

Visit us online at RLBfineart.com for more information or to contact the artist.

Illuminations of the World's Greatest Sermon

The Sermon on the Mount

As Illustrated by Artist
Richard L Burris

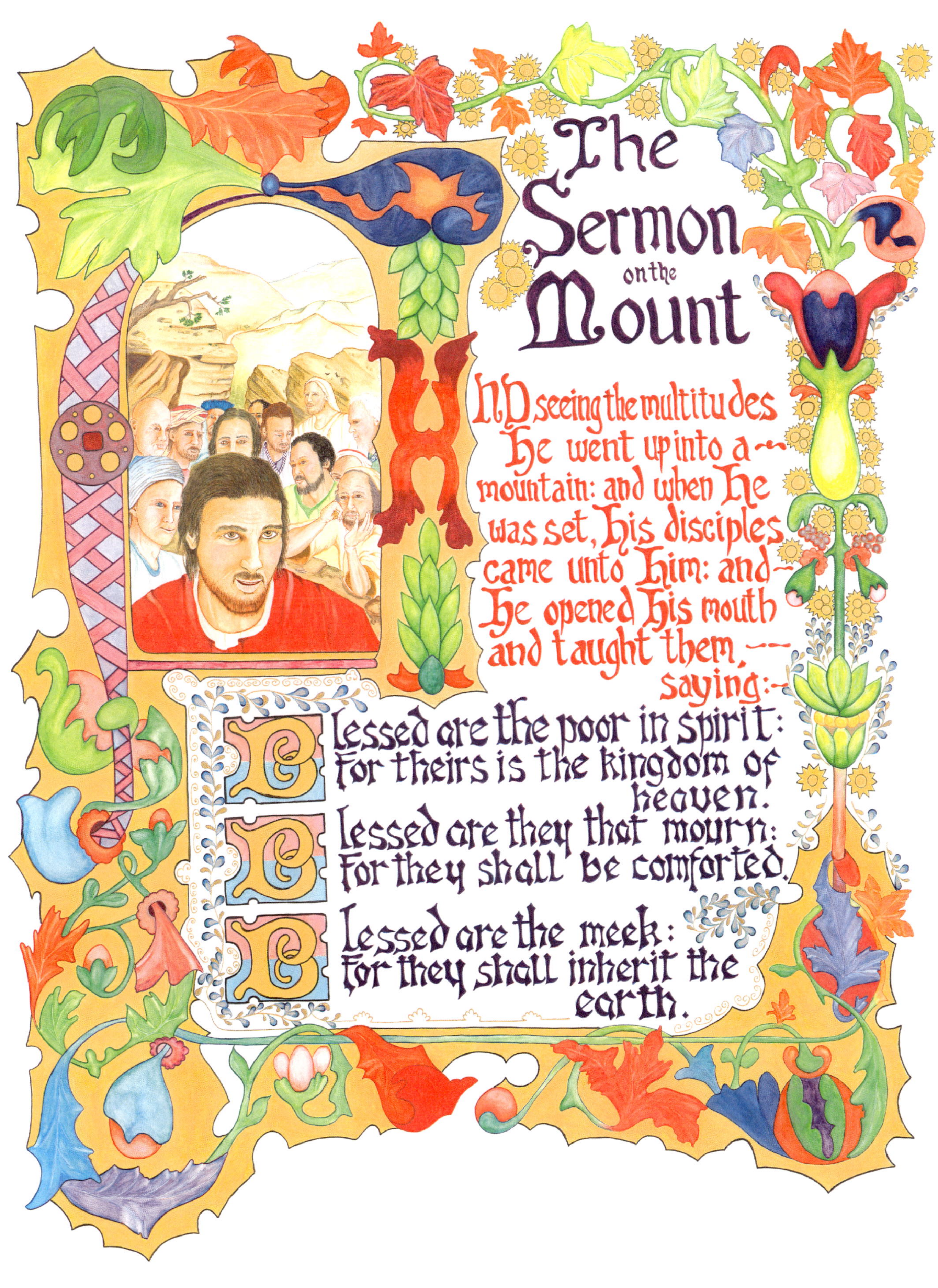

The
Sermon
on the
Mount

AND, seeing the multitudes
He went up into a
mountain: and when He
was set, His disciples
came unto Him: and
He opened His mouth
and taught them,
saying:—

Blessed are the poor in spirit:
For theirs is the kingdom of
heaven.
Blessed are they that mourn:
For they shall be comforted.

Blessed are the meek:
For they shall inherit the
earth.

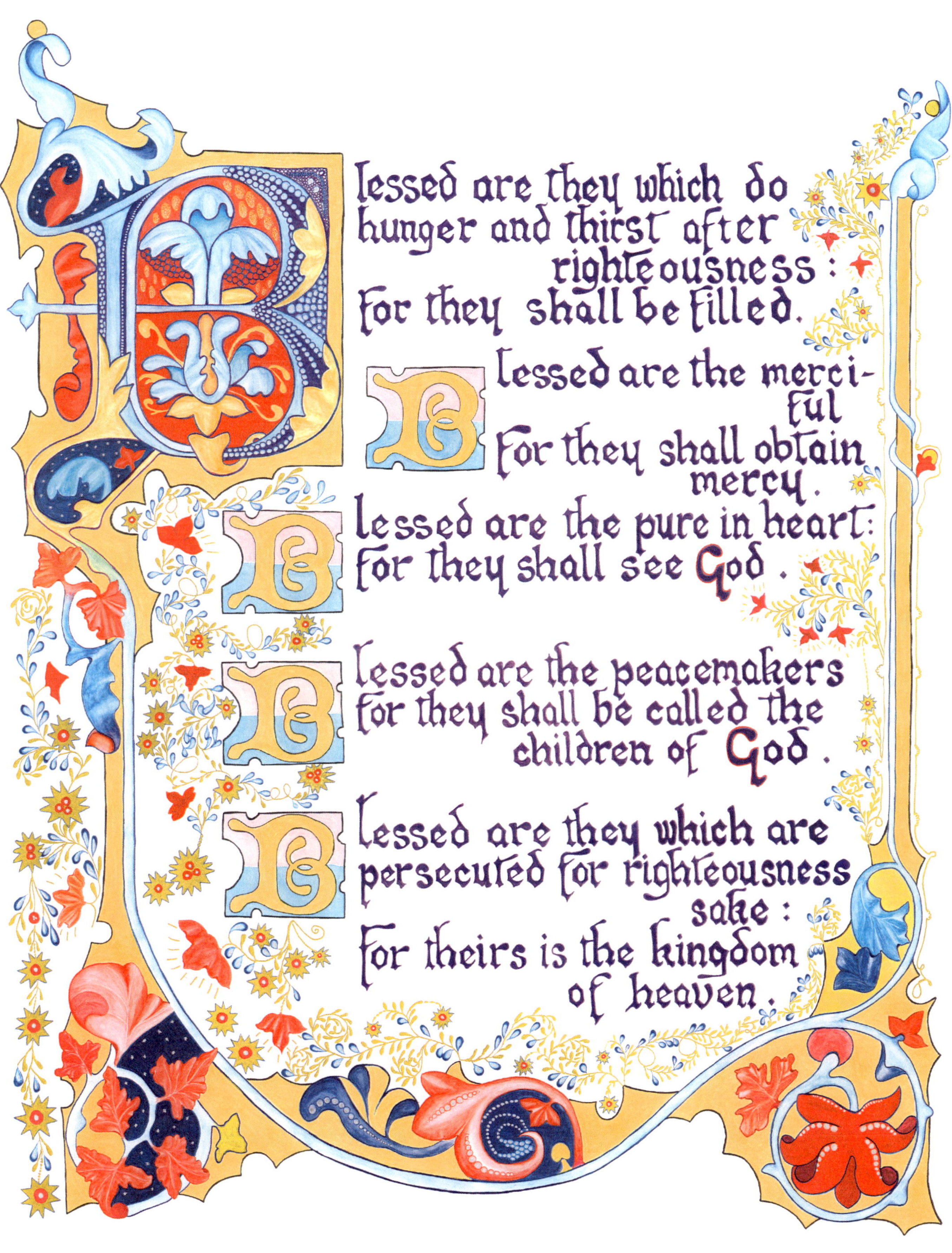
Blessed are they which do hunger and thirst after righteousness: for they shall be filled.
Blessed are the merciful For they shall obtain mercy.
Blessed are the pure in heart: for they shall see God.
Blessed are the peacemakers for they shall be called the children of God.
Blessed are they which are persecuted for righteousness sake: For theirs is the kingdom of heaven.

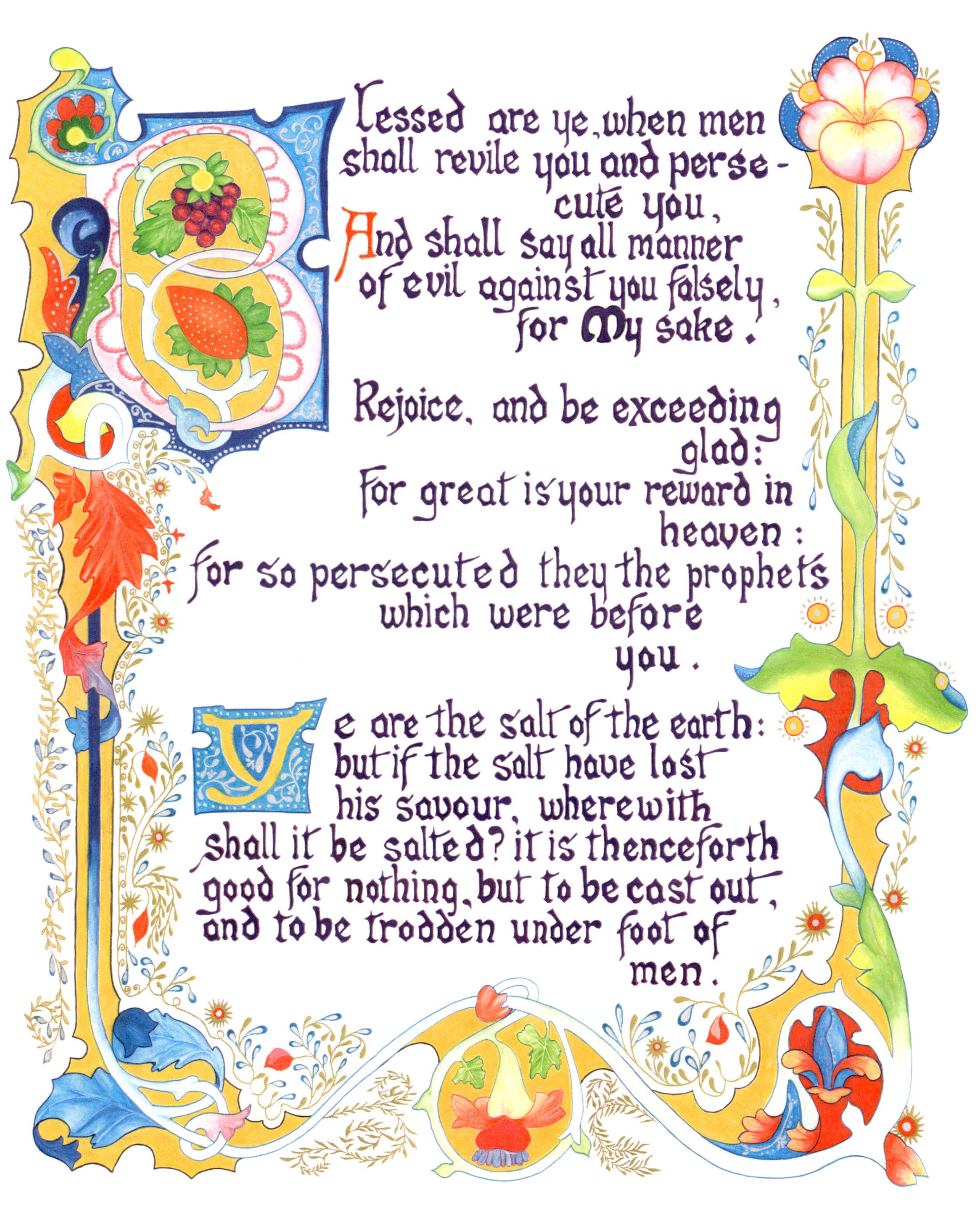

Blessed are ye, when men
shall revile you and persecute you,
And shall say all manner
of evil against you falsely,
for My sake.

Rejoice, and be exceeding
glad:
For great is your reward in
heaven:
for so persecuted they the prophets
which were before
you.

Ye are the salt of the earth:
but if the salt have lost
his savour, wherewith
shall it be salted? it is thenceforth
good for nothing, but to be cast out,
and to be trodden under foot of
men.

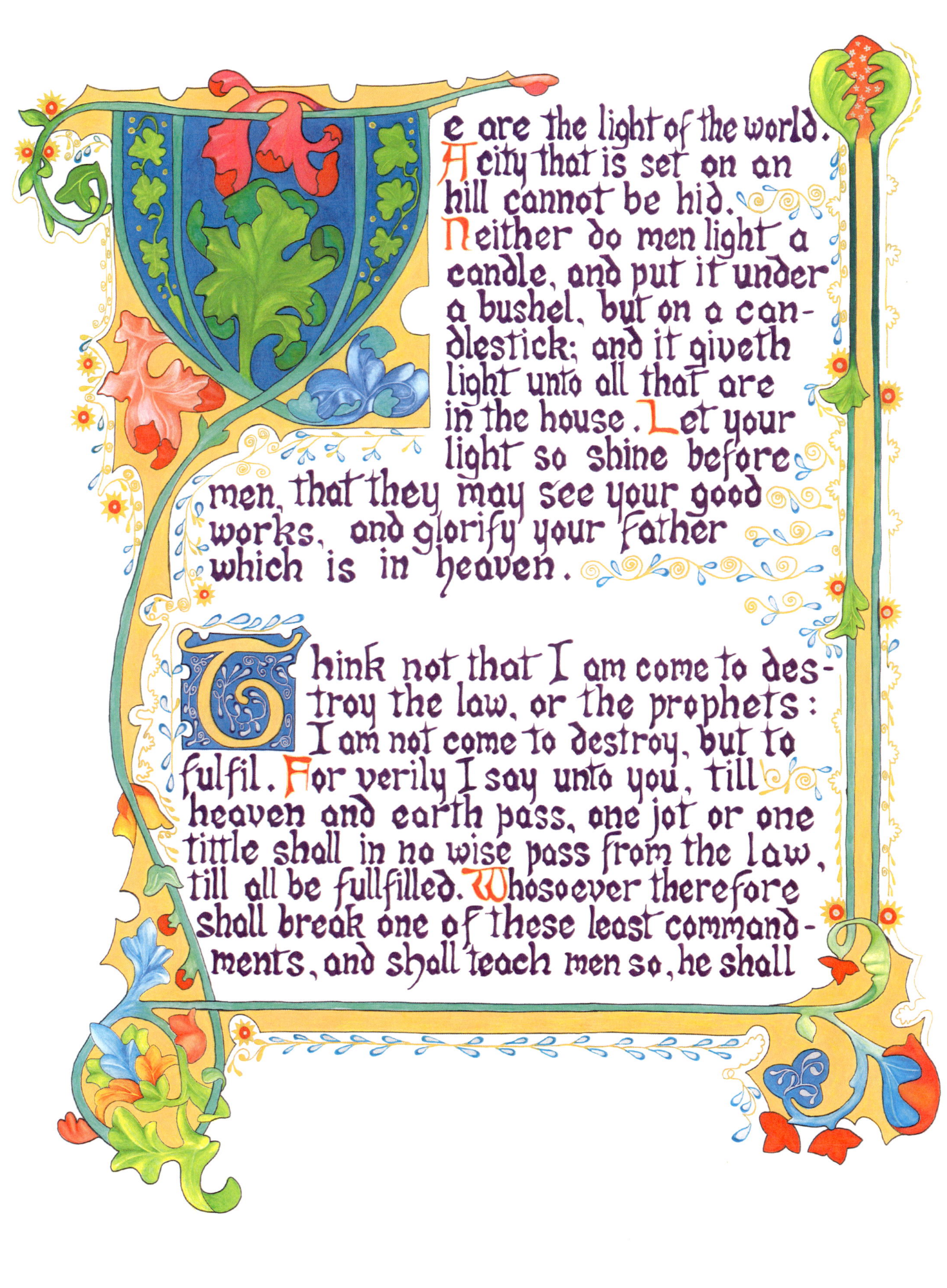

e are the light of the world. A city that is set on an hill cannot be hid. Neither do men light a candle, and put it under a bushel, but on a candlestick; and it giveth light unto all that are in the house. Let your light so shine before men, that they may see your good works, and glorify your Father which is in heaven.

Think not that I am come to destroy the law, or the prophets: I am not come to destroy, but to fulfil. For verily I say unto you, till heaven and earth pass, one jot or one tittle shall in no wise pass from the law, till all be fullfilled. Whosoever therefore shall break one of these least commandments, and shall teach men so, he shall

be called the least in the kingdom of heaven: but whosoever shall do and teach them, the same shall be called great in the kingdom of heaven. For I say unto you, that except your righteousness shall exceed the righteousness of the scribes and pharisees, ye shall in no case enter into the kingdom of heaven.

Ye have heard that it was said by them of old time, Thou shalt not kill; and whosoever shall kill shall be in danger of the judgment: but I say unto you, that whosoever is angry with his brother without a cause shall be in danger of the judgement: and whosoever shall say to his brother, Raca shall be in danger of the council: but whosoever shall say, Thou fool, shall be in danger of hell fire. Therefore if thou bring thy gift to the alter and there

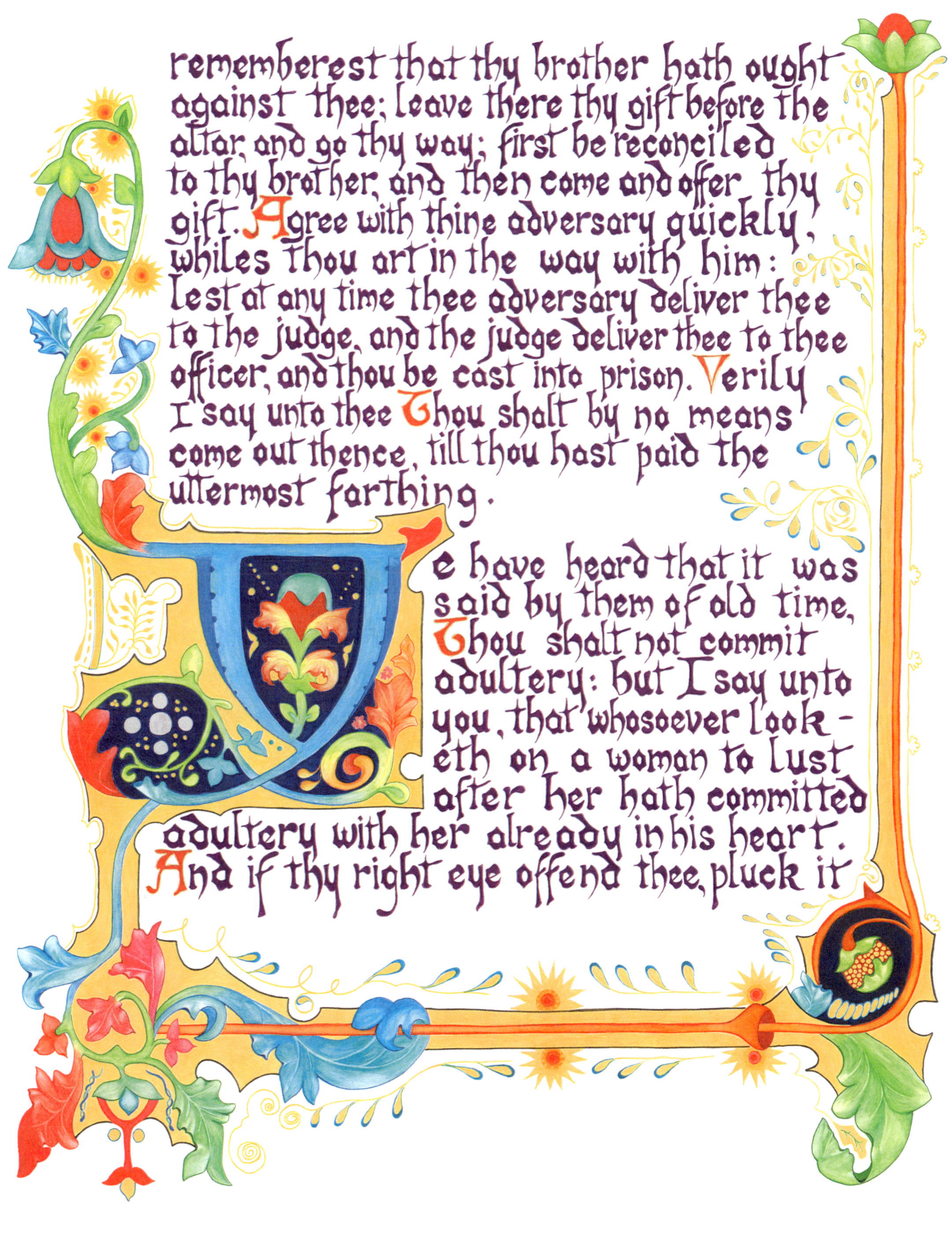

rememberest that thy brother hath ought against thee; leave there thy gift before the altar, and go thy way; first be reconciled to thy brother, and then come and offer thy gift. Agree with thine adversary quickly, whiles thou art in the way with him: lest at any time thee adversary deliver thee to the judge, and the judge deliver thee to thee officer, and thou be cast into prison. Verily I say unto thee Thou shalt by no means come out thence, till thou hast paid the uttermost farthing.

e have heard that it was said by them of old time, Thou shalt not commit adultery: but I say unto you, that whosoever look - eth on a woman to lust after her hath committed adultery with her already in his heart. And if thy right eye offend thee, pluck it

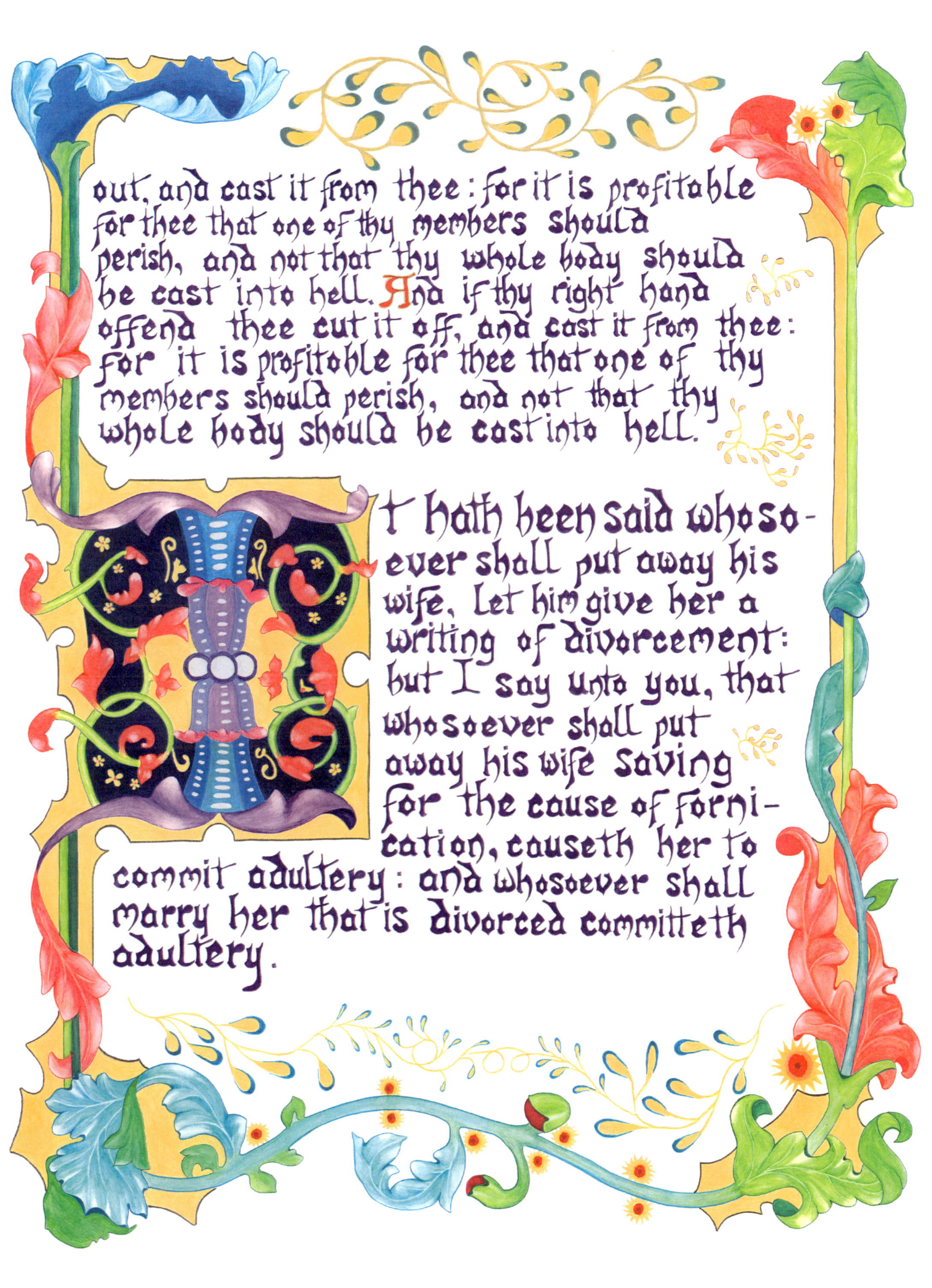

out, and cast it from thee: for it is profitable for thee that one of thy members should perish, and not that thy whole body should be cast into hell. And if thy right hand offend thee cut it off, and cast it from thee: for it is profitable for thee that one of thy members should perish, and not that thy whole body should be cast into hell.

It hath been said whosoever shall put away his wife, Let him give her a writing of divorcement: but I say unto you, that whosoever shall put away his wife saving for the cause of fornication, causeth her to commit adultery: and whosoever shall marry her that is divorced committeth adultery.

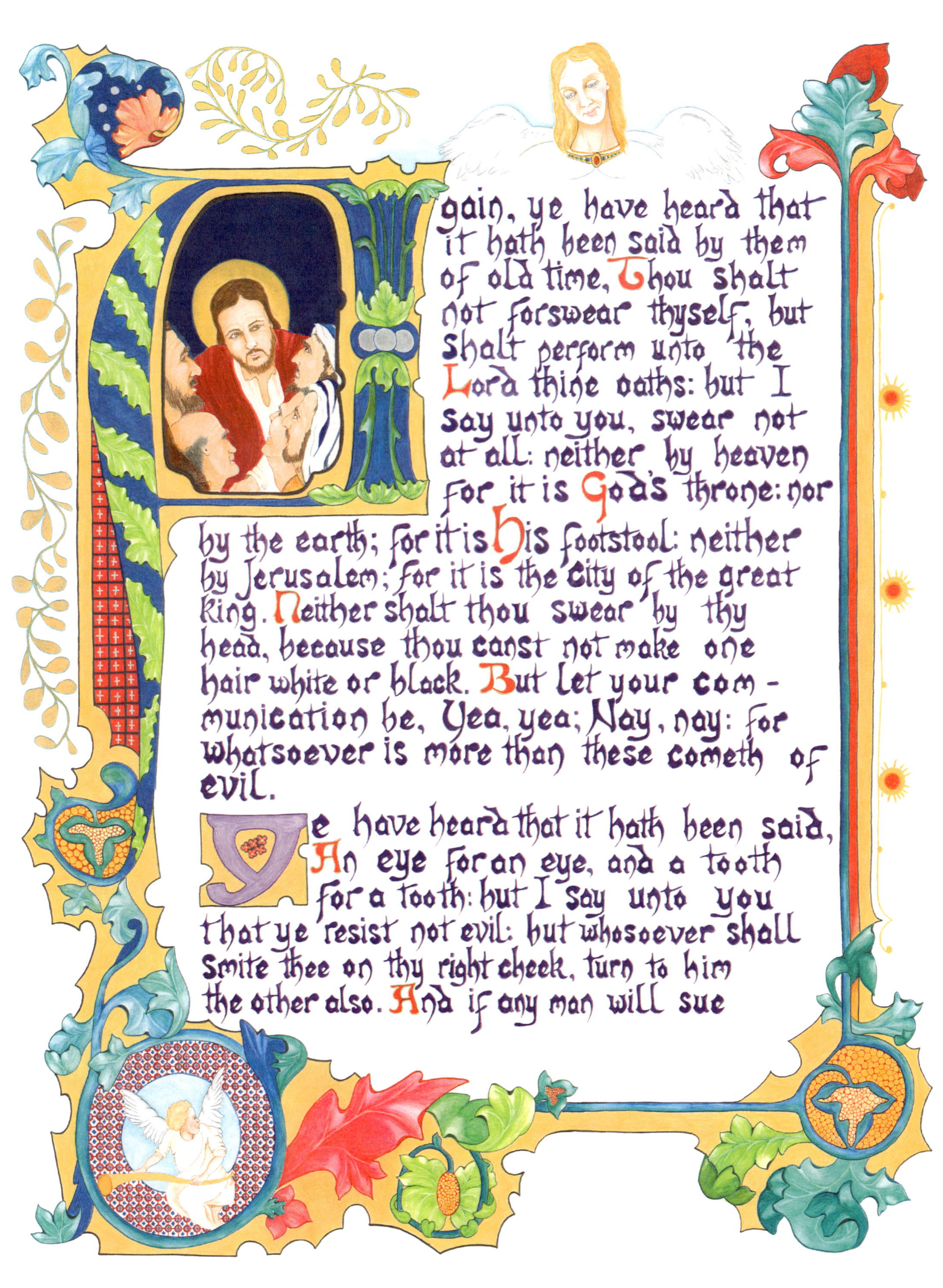

gain, ye have heard that it hath been said by them of old time, Thou shalt not forswear thyself, but shalt perform unto the Lord thine oaths: but I say unto you, swear not at all: neither by heaven for it is God's throne: nor by the earth; for it is His footstool: neither by Jerusalem; for it is the City of the great king. Neither shalt thou swear by thy head, because thou canst not make one hair white or black. But let your communication be, Yea, yea; Nay, nay: for whatsoever is more than these cometh of evil.

e have heard that it hath been said, An eye for an eye, and a tooth for a tooth: but I say unto you that ye resist not evil: but whosoever shall smite thee on thy right cheek, turn to him the other also. And if any man will sue

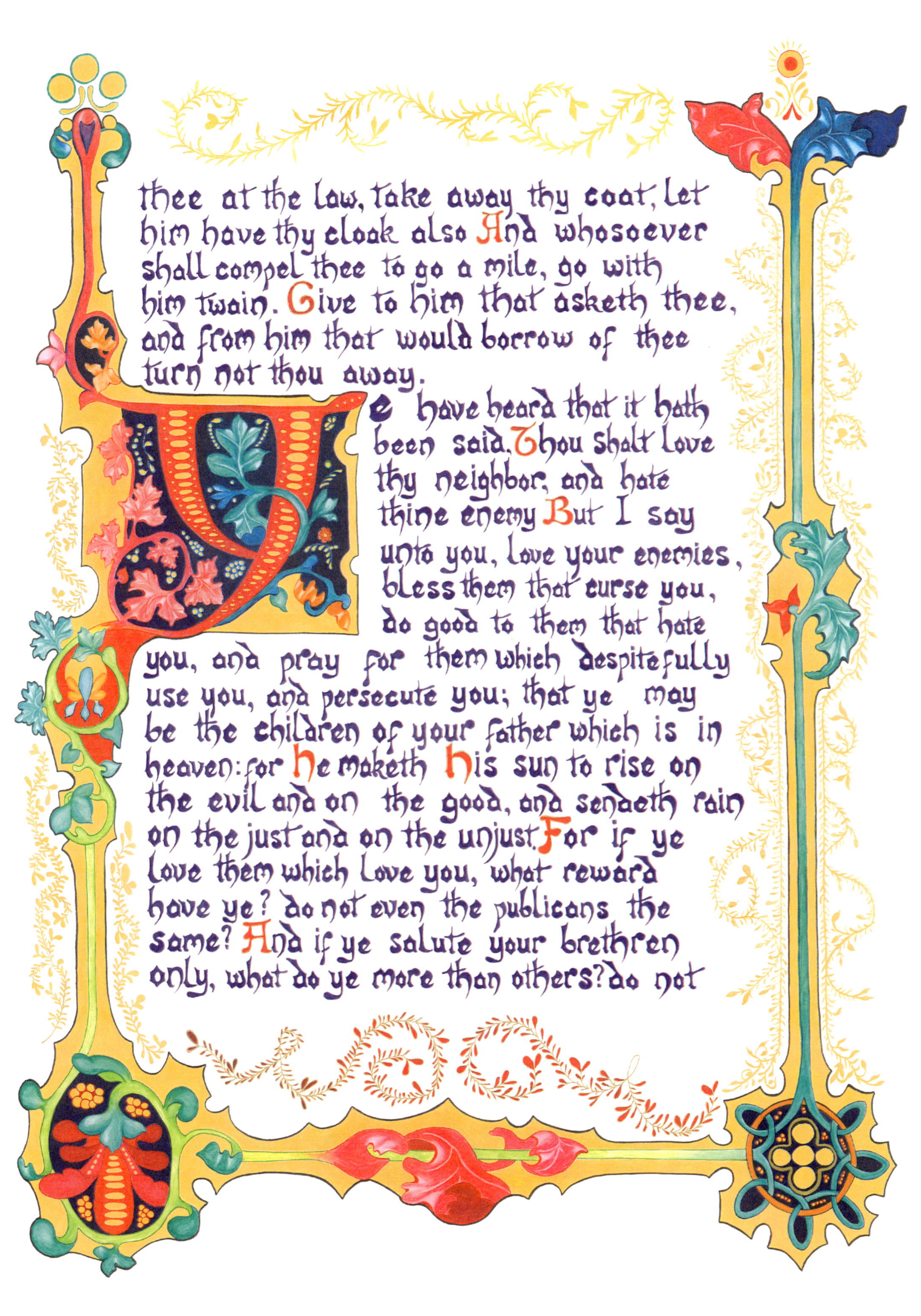

thee at the law, take away thy coat, let him have thy cloak also And whosoever shall compel thee to go a mile, go with him twain. Give to him that asketh thee, and from him that would borrow of thee turn not thou away.

Ye have heard that it hath been said, Thou shalt love thy neighbor, and hate thine enemy But I say unto you, love your enemies, bless them that curse you, do good to them that hate you, and pray for them which despitefully use you, and persecute you; that ye may be the children of your father which is in heaven: for he maketh His sun to rise on the evil and on the good, and sendeth rain on the just and on the unjust. For if ye love them which love you, what reward have ye? do not even the publicans the same? And if ye salute your brethren only, what do ye more than others? do not

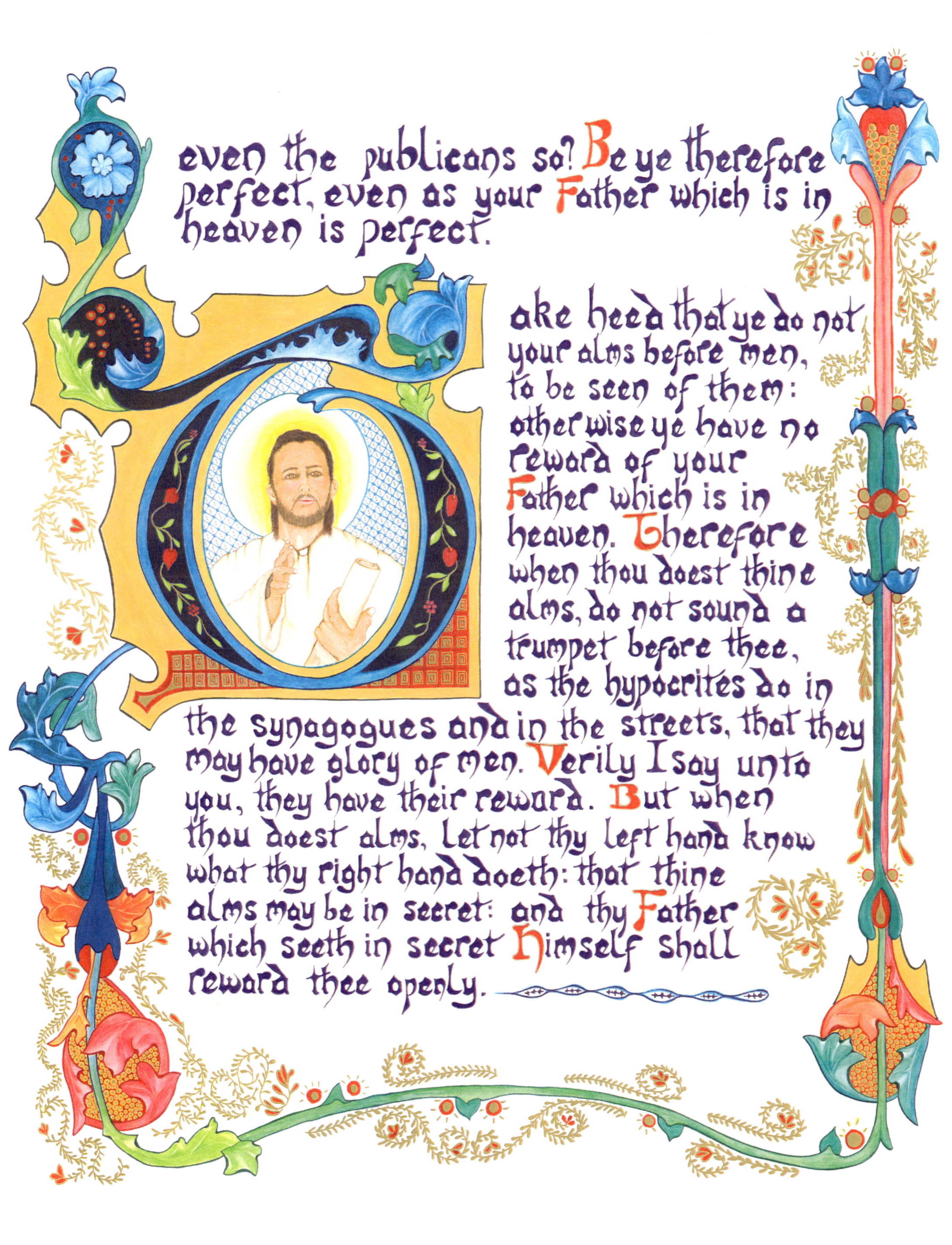even the publicans so? Be ye therefore perfect, even as your Father which is in heaven is perfect.

ake heed that ye do not your alms before men, to be seen of them: otherwise ye have no reward of your Father which is in heaven. Therefore when thou doest thine alms, do not sound a trumpet before thee, as the hypocrites do in the synagogues and in the streets, that they may have glory of men. Verily I say unto you, they have their reward. But when thou doest alms, let not thy left hand know what thy right hand doeth: that thine alms may be in secret: and thy Father which seeth in secret Himself shall reward thee openly.

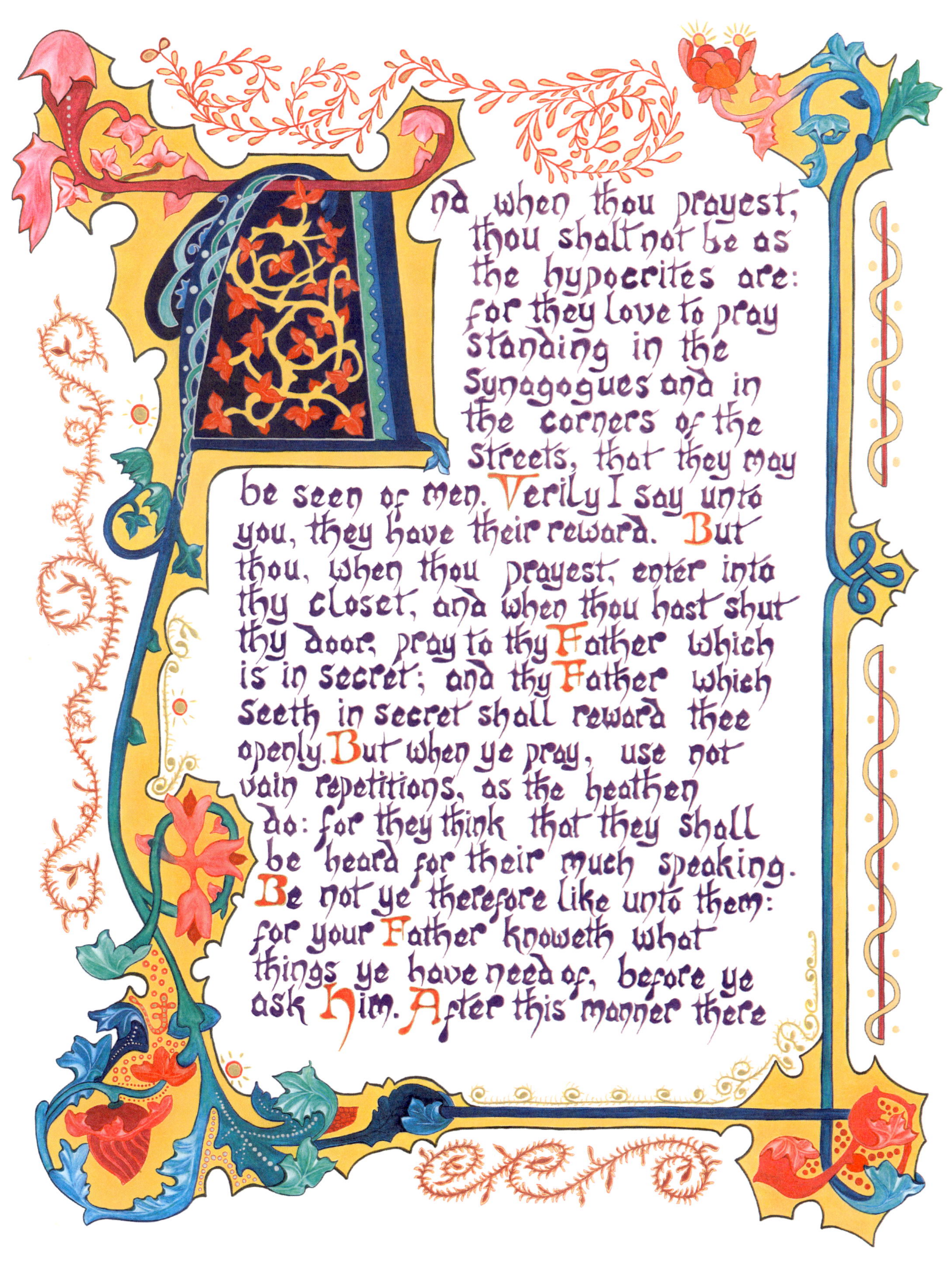

And when thou prayest, thou shalt not be as the hypocrites are: for they love to pray standing in the Synagogues and in the corners of the streets, that they may be seen of men. Verily I say unto you, they have their reward. But thou, when thou prayest, enter into thy closet, and when thou hast shut thy door, pray to thy Father which is in secret; and thy Father which seeth in secret shall reward thee openly. But when ye pray, use not vain repetitions, as the heathen do: for they think that they shall be heard for their much speaking. Be not ye therefore like unto them: for your Father knoweth what things ye have need of, before ye ask Him. After this manner there

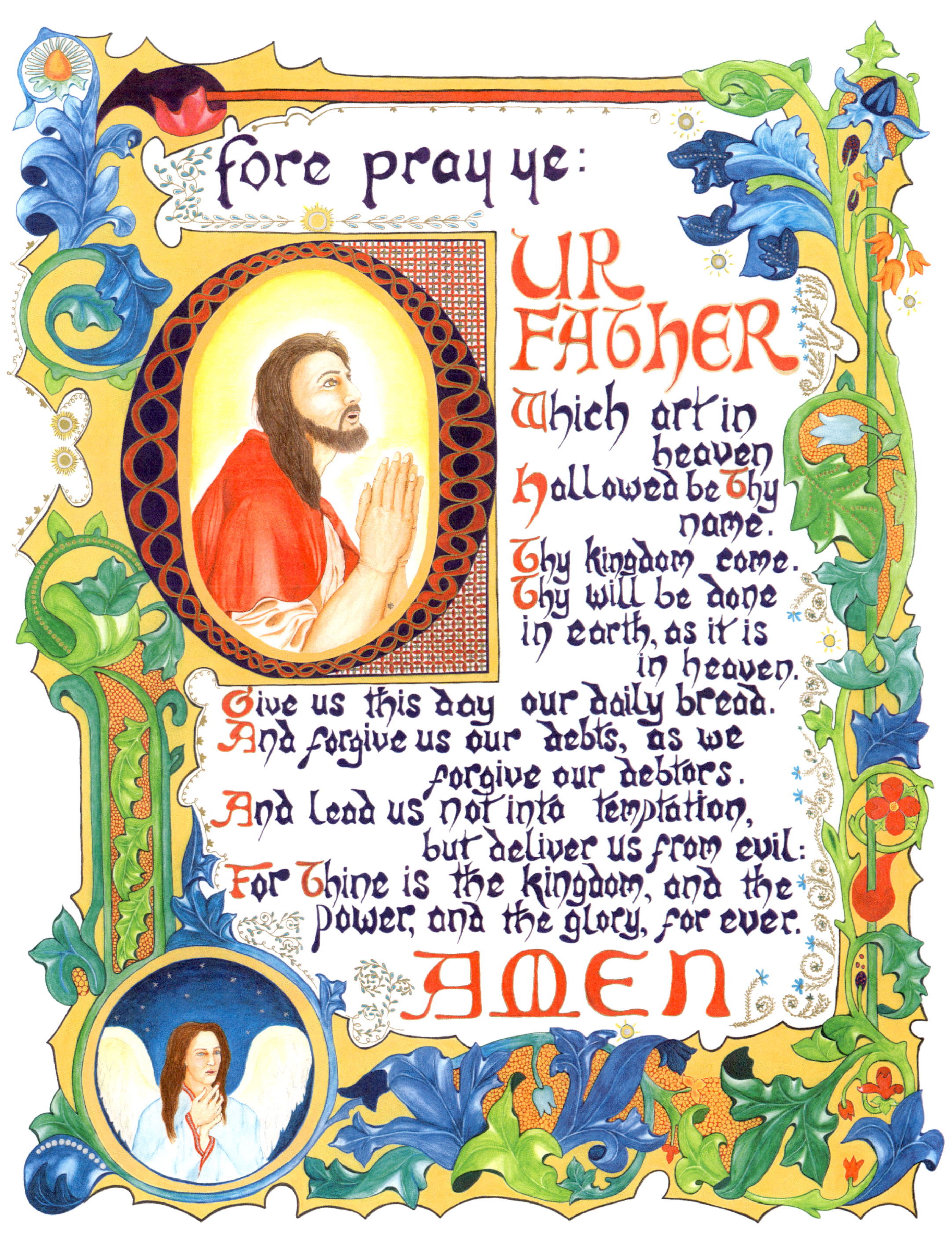

fore pray ye:

UR FATHER
Which art in heaven
Hallowed be Thy name.
Thy kingdom come.
Thy will be done
in earth, as it is
in heaven.
Give us this day our daily bread.
And forgive us our debts, as we
forgive our debtors.
And lead us not into temptation,
but deliver us from evil:
For Thine is the kingdom, and the
power, and the glory, for ever.
AMEN

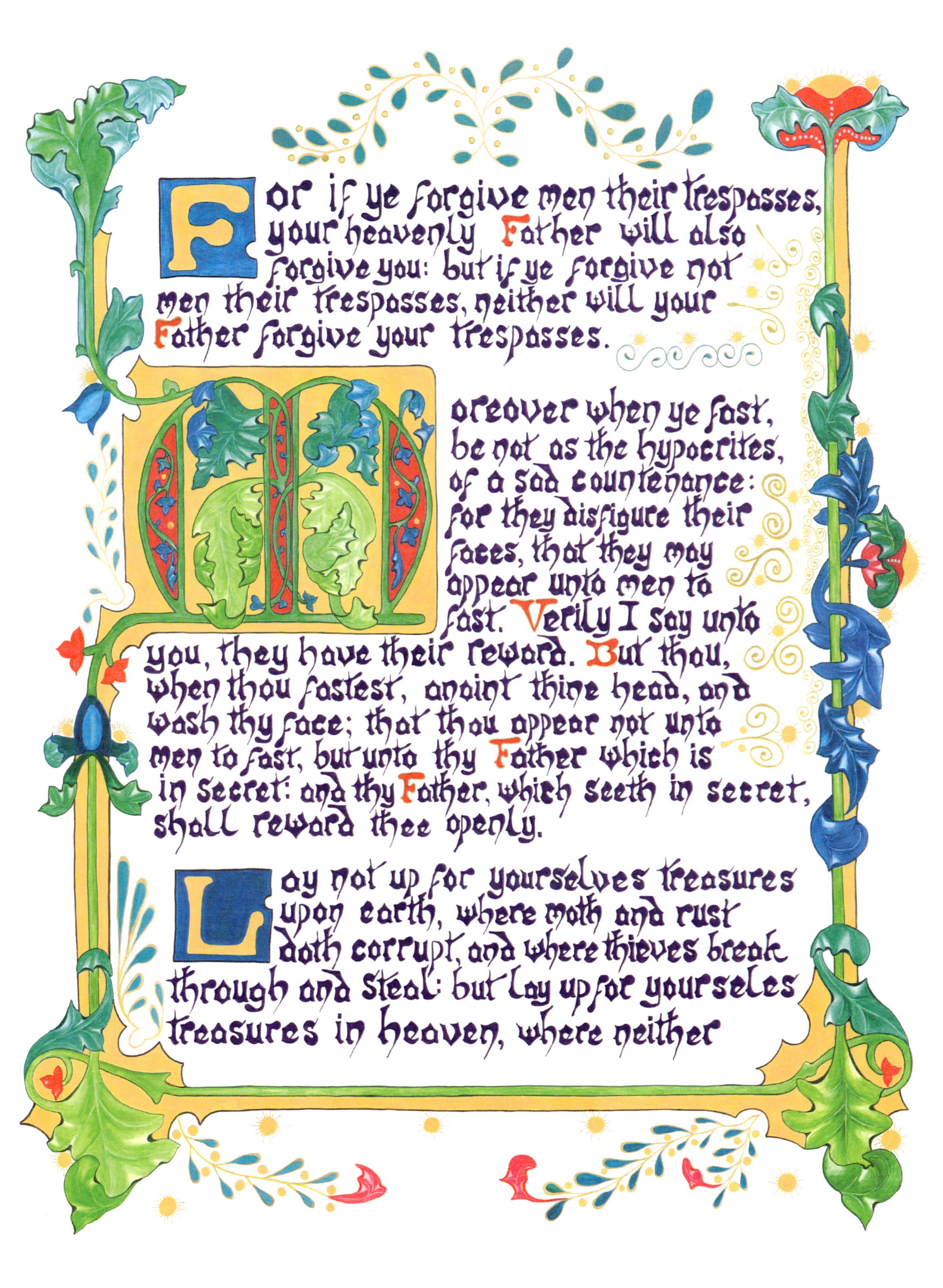

For if ye forgive men their trespasses, your heavenly Father will also forgive you: but if ye forgive not men their trespasses, neither will your Father forgive your trespasses.

Moreover when ye fast, be not as the hypocrites, of a sad countenance: for they disfigure their faces, that they may appear unto men to fast. Verily I say unto you, they have their reward. But thou, when thou fastest, anoint thine head, and wash thy face; that thou appear not unto men to fast, but unto thy Father which is in secret: and thy Father, which seeth in secret, shall reward thee openly.

Lay not up for yourselves treasures upon earth, where moth and rust doth corrupt, and where thieves break through and steal: but lay up for yourseles treasures in heaven, where neither

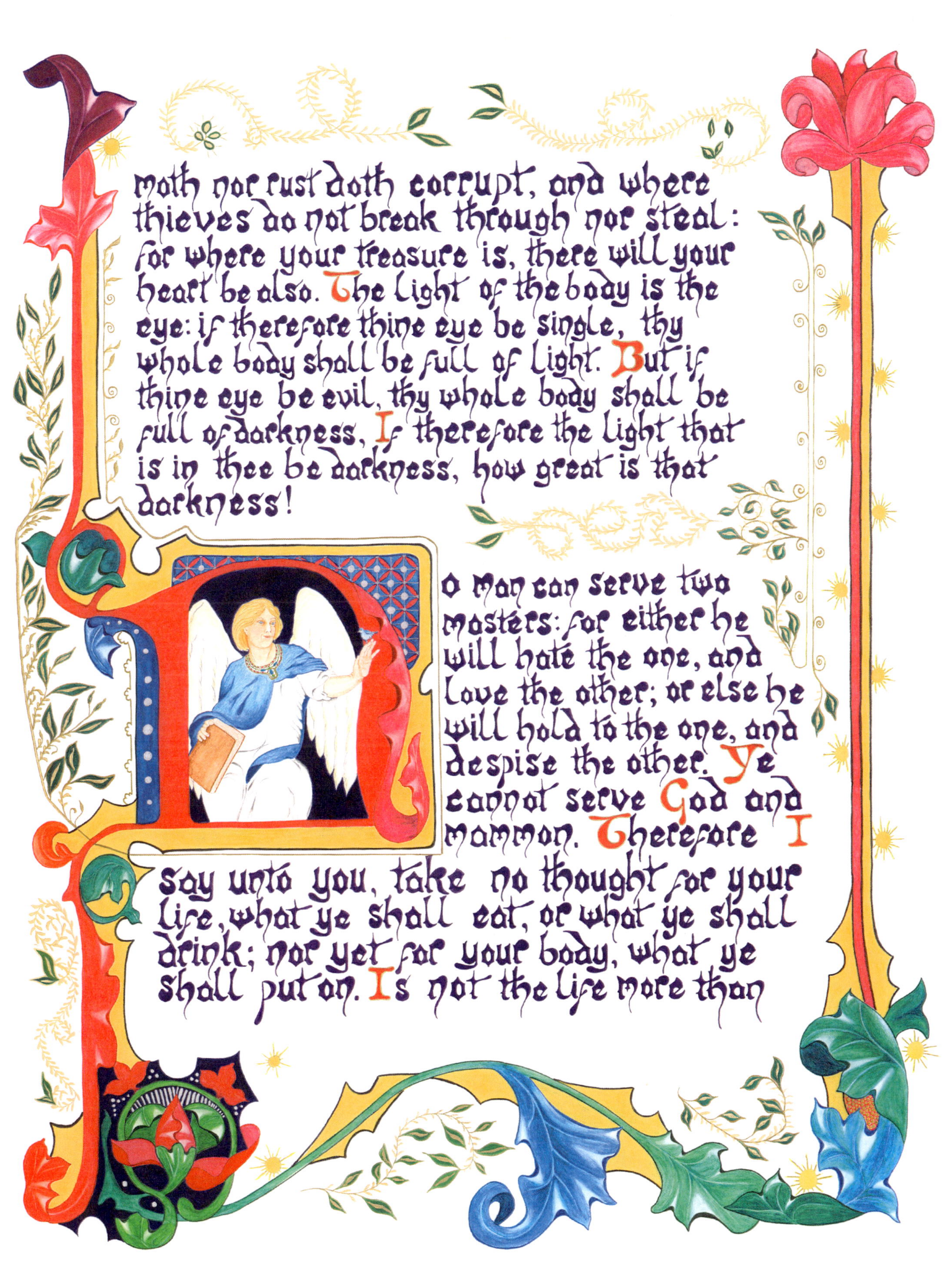

moth nor rust doth corrupt, and where thieves do not break through nor steal: for where your treasure is, there will your heart be also. The light of the body is the eye: if therefore thine eye be single, thy whole body shall be full of light. But if thine eye be evil, thy whole body shall be full of darkness. If therefore the light that is in thee be darkness, how great is that darkness!

No man can serve two masters: for either he will hate the one, and love the other; or else he will hold to the one, and despise the other. Ye cannot serve God and mammon. Therefore I say unto you, take no thought for your life, what ye shall eat, or what ye shall drink; nor yet for your body, what ye shall put on. Is not the life more than

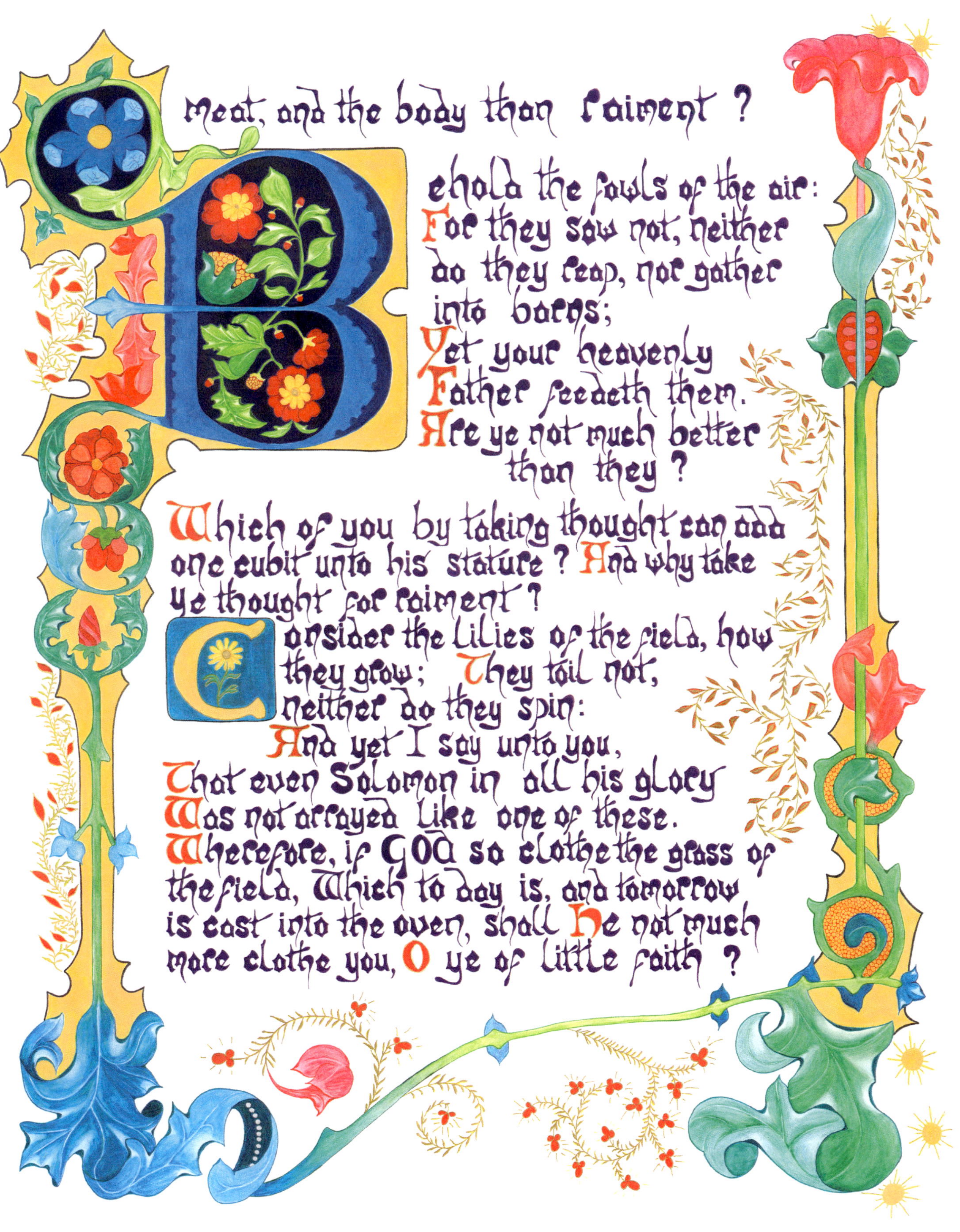

meat, and the body than raiment?

Behold the fowls of the air:
For they sow not, neither
do they reap, nor gather
into barns;
Yet your heavenly
Father feedeth them.
Are ye not much better
than they?

Which of you by taking thought can add
one cubit unto his stature? And why take
ye thought for raiment?
Consider the Lilies of the field, how
they grow; They toil not,
neither do they spin:
And yet I say unto you,
That even Solomon in all his glory
Was not arrayed like one of these.
Wherefore, if GOD so clothe the grass of
the field, Which to day is, and tomorrow
is cast into the oven, shall He not much
more clothe you, O ye of little faith?

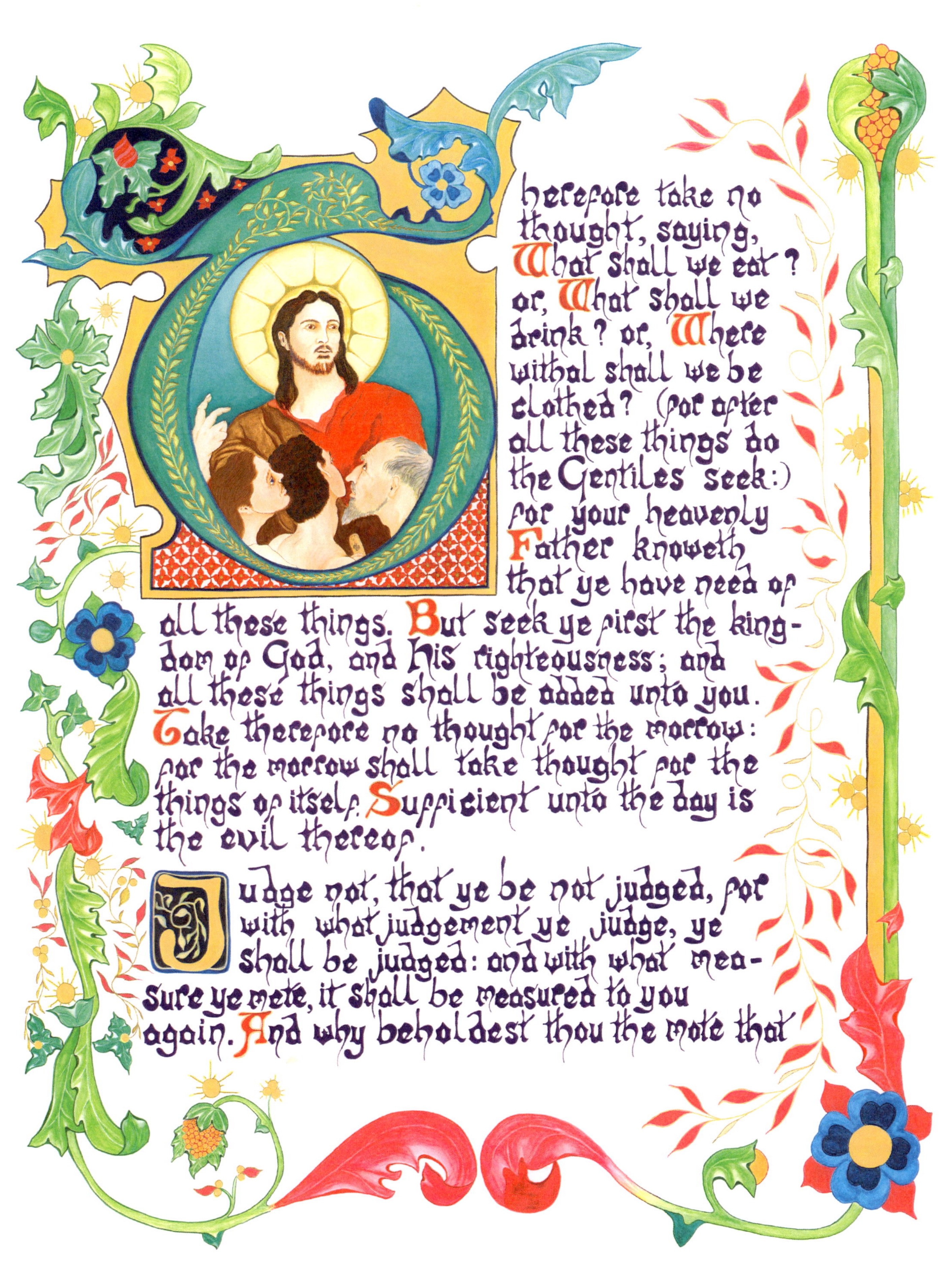

herefore take no thought, saying, What shall we eat? or, What shall we drink? or, Where withal shall we be clothed? (For after all these things do the Gentiles seek:) for your heavenly Father knoweth that ye have need of all these things. But seek ye first the kingdom of God, and His righteousness; and all these things shall be added unto you. Take therefore no thought for the morrow: for the morrow shall take thought for the things of itself. Sufficient unto the day is the evil thereof.

udge not, that ye be not judged. For with what judgement ye judge, ye shall be judged: and with what measure ye mete, it shall be measured to you again. And why beholdest thou the mote that

is in thy brothers eye, but considerest not the beam that is in thine own eye? Or how wilt thou say to thy brother, Let me pull out the mote out of thine eye; and, behold, a beam is in thine own eye? Thou hypocrite, first cast out the beam out of thine own eye; and then shalt thou see clearly to cast out the mote out of thy brothers eye. Give not that which is holy unto the dogs, neither cast ye your pearls before swine, lest they trample them under their feet, and turn again and rend you.

Ask, and it shall be given you; seek, and ye shall find; knock, and it shall be opened unto you. For every one that asketh receiveth; and he that seeketh findeth; and to him that knocketh it shall be opened. Or what man is there of you, whom if his son ask bread, will he give him a stone? Or if he ask a fish, will he give him a serpent? If ye then, being evil, know how to give good gifts unto your children, how much more shall your Father which is in heaven give good things

to them that ask Him? Therefore all things
whatsoever ye would that men should do to
you, do ye even so to them: for this is the
Law and the prophets.

Enter ye in at the strait
gate: for wide is the
gate, and broad is the
way, that leadeth to
destruction, and many
there be which go in
thereat: because strait
is the gate, and narrow is
the way which leadeth
unto life and few there
be that find it.

Beware of false prophets, which come
to you in sheeps clothing, but inward-
ly they are ravening wolves.
Ye shall know them by their fruits. Do
men gather grapes of thorns, or figs of
thistles? Even so every good tree bringeth
forth good fruit; but a corrupt tree bringeth

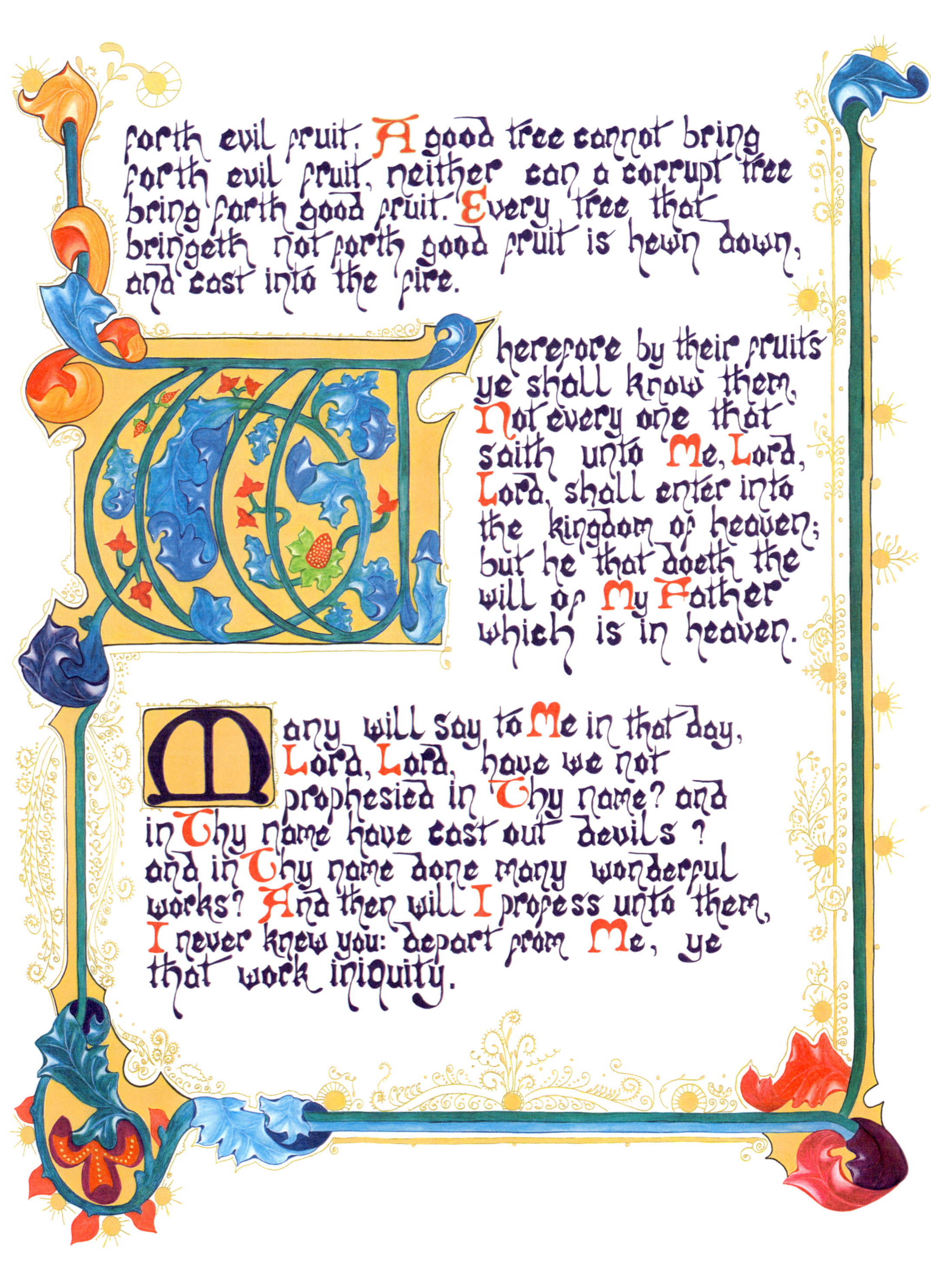

forth evil fruit. A good tree cannot bring forth evil fruit, neither can a corrupt tree bring forth good fruit. Every tree that bringeth not forth good fruit is hewn down, and cast into the fire.

Therefore by their fruits ye shall know them. Not every one that saith unto Me, Lord, Lord, shall enter into the kingdom of heaven; but he that doeth the will of My Father which is in heaven.

Many will say to Me in that day, Lord, Lord, have we not prophesied in Thy name? and in Thy name have cast out devils? and in Thy name done many wonderful works? And then will I profess unto them, I never knew you: depart from Me, ye that work iniquity.

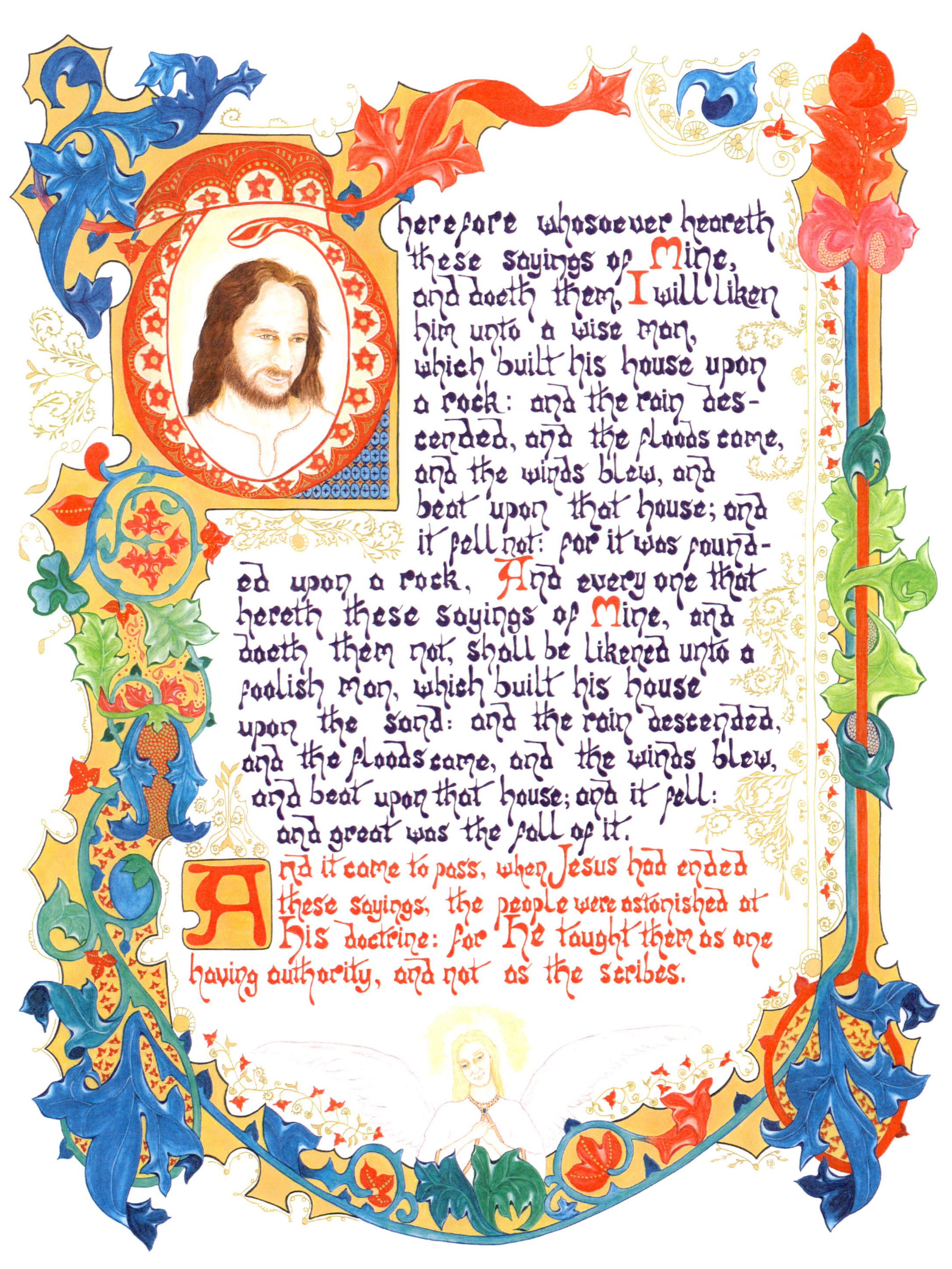

Therefore whosoever heareth these sayings of Mine, and doeth them, I will liken him unto a wise man, which built his house upon a rock: and the rain descended, and the floods came, and the winds blew, and beat upon that house; and it fell not: for it was founded upon a rock, And every one that heareth these sayings of Mine, and doeth them not, shall be likened unto a foolish man, which built his house upon the sand: and the rain descended, and the floods came, and the winds blew, and beat upon that house; and it fell: and great was the fall of it.

And it came to pass, when Jesus had ended these sayings, the people were astonished at His doctrine: for He taught them as one having authority, and not as the scribes.

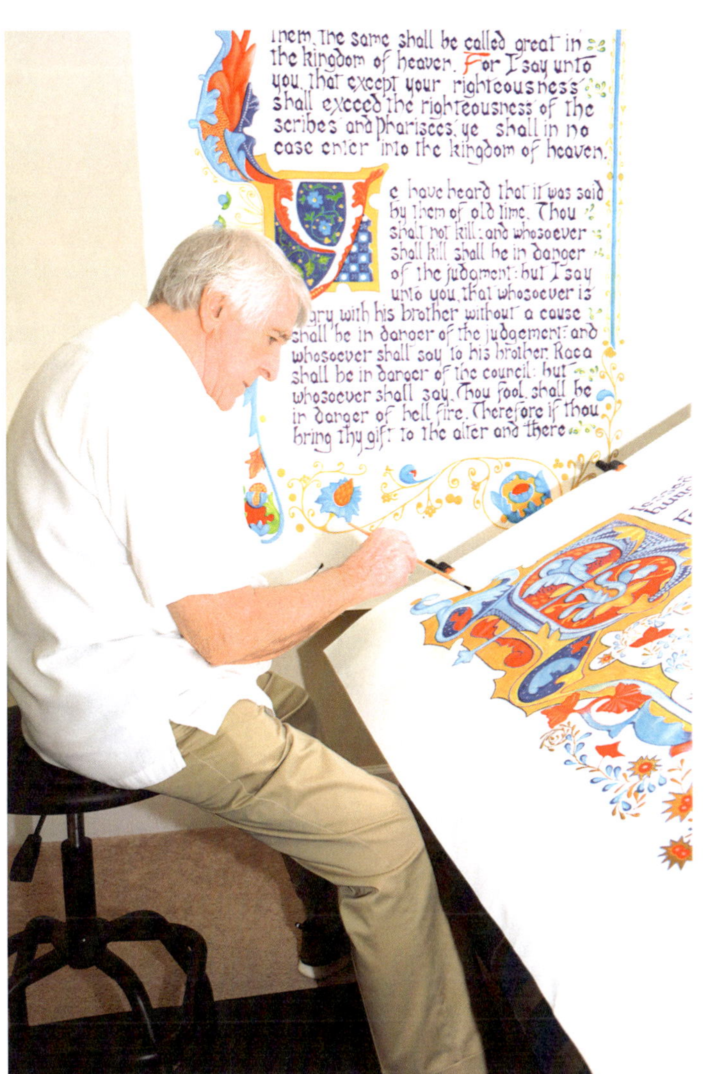

Artist Richard L Burris
working on his Illuminations Series

Richard, a resident of South Florida since 2001, was born in a small, southwest Missouri community. It was there he spent his youth enjoying the beauty and learning the values of a rural lifestyle. It was also where he first discovered his love of art.

Intrigued with the biblical illuminations in a book given to him one Christmas when he was still a boy, he vowed to paint some of his own one day. This collection is a testament to his will and his lifelong dream, and showcases his series which he finally completed 74 years after his initial exposure to his life-changing gift.

The full story behind his inspiration can be found on the next page.

If you would like archival quality reproductions of his beautiful work, they are available in a variety of sizes and can be printed on multiple types of media, including water-color paper and aluminum. Please visit him online at RLBfineart.com for more information.

Richard's skillful work of 20 pieces comprising his Illuminations series is larger than life. These 4 x 5 foot originals are first Illustrated, and then finished with stunning watercolors and inks in vibrant hues and tones. Even the lettering is all pain-stakingly done by hand, the way the old masters used to do it. Four years in the making, his gorgeous series is ready to be shared with the world.

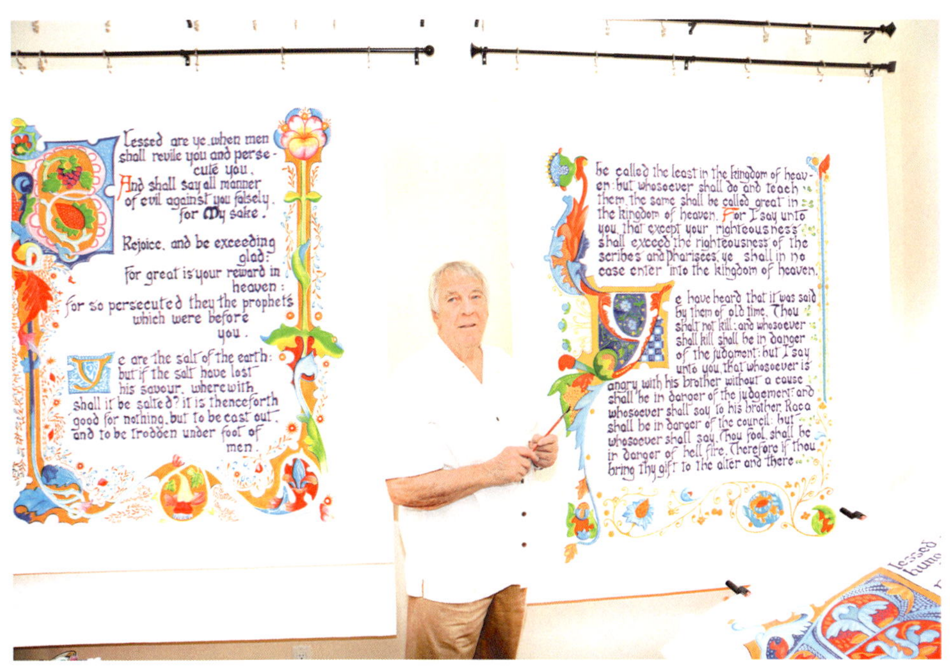

Artist Richard L Burris with Illuminations

In the spring of 1950, after losing a younger brother to leukemia, my family moved from the rental holding his memories, into an even smaller rental within the same tiny town in Southwest Missouri. Across the dirt street sat an abandoned old house similar to ours.

An elderly lady moved into this rundown property. A pickup truck unloaded what little furniture and belongings she possessed and I spied her settling into a rocker on her porch. She was glaring at her yard full of tall weeds and an assortment of scattered debris.

While watching and wondering about her, my mother grabbed me with one hand and marched me across the street, onto her porch, and in front of the startled woman.

After introducing herself, my mother said, "This is my son, Dickie. He'll be taking care of your yard and any errands that you need done. Don't pay him anything. What he learns will be payment enough. Besides, it'll keep him out of trouble this summer."

That was the beginning of the most memorable relationship I ever cherished. Ms. Carrie Taylor and I became quite fond of one another and enjoyed one another's company daily until an incident in September of that year. I never knew what transpired, but she suddenly no longer wanted my company and began avoiding me completely. It was very upsetting.

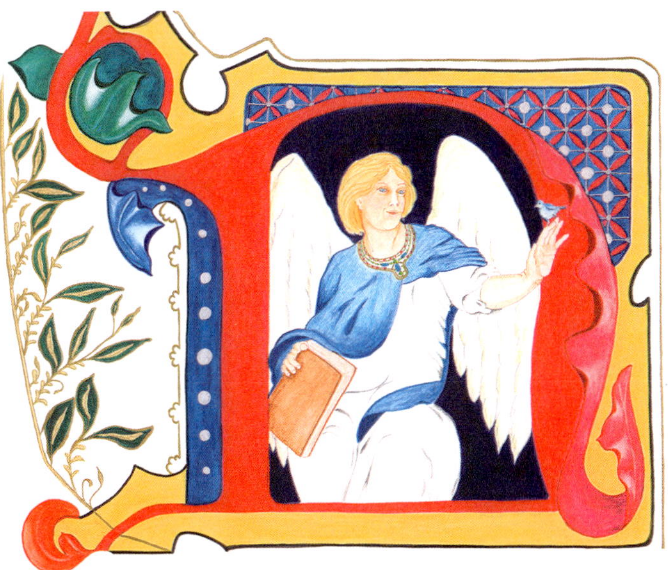

In October, I became ill with something unknown—and never identified—and I spent the next few months in bed with almost daily visits from our doctor. Sadly, there was no contact or word of any kind from Ms. Taylor, until that Christmas Eve, when I woke to find her at my bedside. She told me how much she had missed me, and that I was never out of her thoughts or prayers, then presented me with a Christmas present and left.

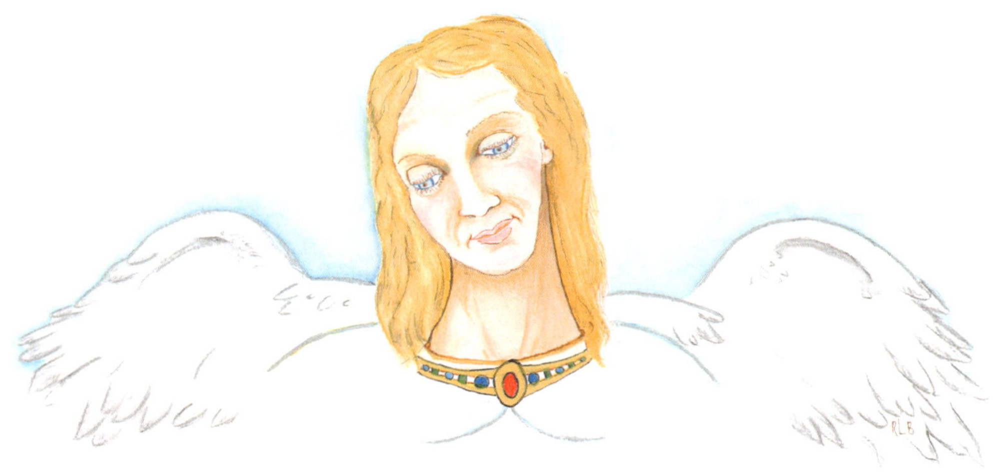

It was a brief, awkward and confusing visit, after which I opened her gift to me. At first, I was disappointed that it was not a toy or game, but a small book titled, *The Words of Jesus.* I became fascinated, however, with the illuminations contained within of Christ's Sermon on the Mount. I studied not the words, but the artwork, which was badly out of registration by the printer, and very difficult to see. I developed a desire to create my own interpretation and what I thought would be an improvement to the work some monk had long ago created. I vowed to do so.

Blessed with artistic talent, life got in the way of ever pursuing my gift. Military service in the Air Force, was followed by a beautiful wife and two sons, and of course, the need for jobs to support them. Retirement gave me time to finally draw and paint, and I spent several years creating artworks for my wife. She passed away in 2019 after a long illness, and after grieving, I began throwing myself into my art once more.

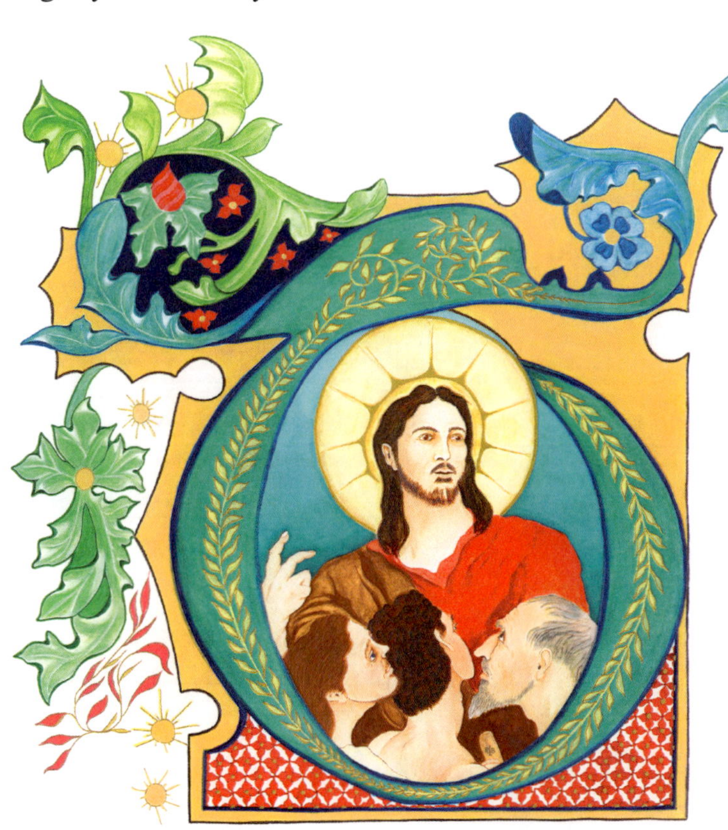

Seventy-four years after receiving that book from my neighbor, and with renewed determination, I have now completed my own illuminations, keeping my vow. A series of twenty watercolor and ink works of art in bold and brilliant colors is ready to be shared with the world.

Richard L Burris

9 781964 962009